IT'S A DIGITAL WORLD!

Amazing
App Developers

Heather C. Hudak

Checkerboard
Library

An Imprint of Abdo Publishing
abdopublishing.com

ABDOPUBLISHING.COM

Published by Abdo Publishing, a division of ABDO, PO Box 398166, Minneapolis, Minnesota 55439. Copyright © 2019 by Abdo Consulting Group, Inc. International copyrights reserved in all countries. No part of this book may be reproduced in any form without written permission from the publisher. Checkerboard Library™ is a trademark and logo of Abdo Publishing.

Printed in the United States of America, North Mankato, Minnesota
052018
092018

 THIS BOOK CONTAINS RECYCLED MATERIALS

Design: Kelly Doudna, Mighty Media, Inc.
Production: Mighty Media, Inc.
Editor: Liz Salzmann
Cover Photographs: iStockphoto (right), Shutterstock (left)
Interior Photographs: AP Images, pp. 17, 18, 21, 23, 28 (top), 28 (bottom), 29 (bottom); iStockphoto, pp. 7, 12, 15; Shutterstock, pp. 4, 9, 11, 24, 25, 27, 29 (top)

Library of Congress Control Number: 2017961586

Publisher's Cataloging-in-Publication Data
Name: Hudak, Heather C., author.
Title: Amazing app developers / by Heather C. Hudak.
Description: Minneapolis, Minnesota : Abdo Publishing, 2019. | Series: It's a digital world! | Includes online resources and index.
Identifiers: ISBN 9781532115301 (lib.bdg.) | ISBN 9781532156021 (ebook)
Subjects: LCSH: Mobile apps--Juvenile literature. | Application software--Development--Juvenile literature. | Occupations--Careers--Jobs--Juvenile literature.
Classification: DDC 005.25--dc23

CONTENTS

Apps Are Everywhere 5

What Is an App Developer? 6

What an App Developer Does .8

App Software 10

App Developer Jobs 12

App Beginnings 14

The iPhone Effect 18

More Markets 20

App Success 22

App Future 26

Timeline 28

Glossary 30

Online Resources 31

Index 32

APPS ARE EVERYWHERE

It's a rainy Saturday. You check the weather on your smartphone. It says it's going to rain all day. You pass the time playing Angry Birds. Later, you're watching YouTube videos on your tablet when a classmate sends you a message. She asks you to work on a school project with her. You open Google Classroom on your laptop and start **collaborating**.

All of these activities are examples of things you can do using **software** applications, or apps. You can use apps on nearly any computer, web **browser**, smartphone, or **mobile** device. There are apps for just about everything, from playing music to buying clothes to tracking airplane flights.

App developers are the people who design and build the cool apps you use every day. They are always coming up with new ideas to make electronic devices even more useful and fun. Have you thought of becoming an app developer?

CHAPTER 1
WHAT IS AN APP DEVELOPER?

App developers create, design, develop, and test apps. They make games, word processors, and other applications for computers and **mobile** devices. Many app developers enjoy building things and have lots of creative ideas. They look for ways to solve problems, make life easier, or just have fun using apps.

Most app developers have a college degree in computer science, **software** engineering, or mobile application development. They usually have a strong interest in math and science and like to solve problems. Designing an app requires excellent planning and attention to detail. App developers need to think about every possible way people will want to use an app. Then they make sure the app can do those things.

There are many elements that go into building an app. So, app developers sometimes work with people who **specialize** in other fields. These people may include software and data

The average salary for an app developer is about $70,000 to 90,000 per year.

specialists to make the app function the way it should. **Graphic** designers help make sure the app looks good. Subject matter experts understand the industry an app is being designed for. They make sure the app meets the needs of the people who will be using it. Although many people **collaborate** on producing an app, it all begins with the app developer.

CHAPTER 2

WHAT AN APP DEVELOPER DOES

App developers can work in different ways. Sometimes they come up with their own ideas for apps. Other times they work for a company or client that has a special need.

An app developer spends a lot of time planning an app and each action it needs to perform. He or she creates flowcharts showing everything the app will do. Only after every detail of the app is planned does the developer start building the app.

Apps run on devices that contain computers. So, a big part of building an app is writing computer **code**. Computer code tells the computer what to do. Computer code has to be very precise. If even a single character is wrong, some or all of the app's functions might not work.

App developers test their work often. Sometimes, they work with

DIGITAL BIT

App developers will sometimes share their computer code. Other people can then use it to build more apps. This is called "open source" software.

App developers often make wireframes when designing apps. These are mock-ups of how the app will look.

people who test apps for them. Then errors in the **code** can be fixed before the app's release.

After the app is released, users can give the developer **feedback**. This could be about problems with using the app. Users can also suggest ideas for improving the app. The developer will then update the app based on the feedback.

CHAPTER 3
APP SOFTWARE

App developers need to know how to use many different types of software. Every computer, smartphone, and tablet has an operating system (OS). This is the software that manages all of the applications and **hardware** on a computer or device. The OS performs tasks such as organizing files, connecting to printers and **networks**, and running apps.

Microsoft Windows, Apple macOS, Apple iOS, and Google Android are examples of OSs. Some apps work on one OS, while others work on more than one. Before building an app, the developer needs to know which OSs it will need to run on.

App developers build apps with programming languages that the OSs can understand. Two commonly used ones are Python and Java. They are cross-platform. This means an app can be built on one OS and run on one or more other OSs. Spotify and YouTube use Python. Java is the official language for Android development.

There are hundreds of coding languages. New programming languages are being developed all the time.

Another programming language used for apps is HTML5. Apps built with HTML5 are web based. This means they are run by internet **browsers**, rather than by the OS directly. Web-based apps work on any OS that has an internet browser, such as Safari, Google Chrome, or Firefox. For example, Google Docs is a web-based app built using HTML5.

CHAPTER 4

APP DEVELOPER JOBS

Many companies hire app developers. Some, such as Amazon and Google, are really big. An app developer at these companies could be just one of many people working on a team. Team members **collaborate** on ideas. Then each person works on one aspect of an app, such as the **code** or **graphic** design.

Communication skills are very important for an app developer. Each person on a team needs to be able to talk clearly about their ideas for the app. And they need to listen to other people's ideas so they can successfully work together.

Google's headquarters is in Mountain View, California. The company is consistently ranked as the best workplace in the world.

A smaller company might have just one app developer. This app developer consults with other people in the company about what the company's apps should do. Then he or she designs and develops the apps. Other app developers don't work for a company at all. Instead, these app developers come up with their own ideas and create independent apps.

Many large **technology** companies, such as Apple and Android, offer app development **software** to the public. These programs are called integrated development **environments** (IDEs). An IDE includes the basic tools an app developer needs to design, build, and test an app. Anyone can use these programs to build apps.

MOBILE APP DEVELOPERS

Mobile app developers build apps for devices such as smartphones and tablets. There are many challenges to creating apps for these devices. The apps need to work and look good on different screen sizes and different mobile OSs. Mobile apps also must use less memory and battery power than apps for computers. And people use mobile devices by touching the screens, rather than using separate keyboards and mice. The buttons and other elements on the screen need to be easy to see and tap.

CHAPTER 5
APP BEGINNINGS

Whether working at companies or independently, app developers have only been around since the 1980s. This is when the first devices with apps came out. These devices were called personal digital assistants (PDAs).

PDAs were handheld computers that had simple operating systems and a few apps. PDA apps helped users do tasks that human assistants would normally do. These included putting events in a calendar, creating documents, and sending emails.

In the 1990s, cell phones with apps started being introduced. Each company that built a new cell phone wanted to outdo its competitors. Companies started adding games and other features to their phones to attract customers. These were the first phone apps. At this time, apps were part of a cell phone's OS. They came on the phone and people couldn't add more.

A **breakthrough** in app development came in 1997 from electronics company Nokia. Nokia had just developed a new cell

The Motorola DynaTAC 8000x was the first cell phone available to the public. It was released in 1983 and cost $3,995!

phone OS. The company wanted to add something fun for people to do with their phones. It decided to include a game app on its phones.

Nokia **software** developer Taneli Armanto created the game. It was no easy task. People were used to computer games that had music, sound effects, and colorful **graphics**. This type of game would require way too much memory to fit on the phone's OS.

Armanto would need to make a game that was just as interesting and fun to play, but had fewer features. The developer faced other challenges too. The phone had a low-resolution screen and slow processor speed. This meant the game had to be simple.

Armanto decided to adapt popular video game Blockade for the Nokia phone. He called the new game Snake. In the game, players used the phone's number pad keys to move a snake into little squares. The squares represented food. Each time the snake entered a square, it got bigger. Snake was a hit! People instantly became addicted to the concept of **mobile** games.

A new **technology** standard was developed in 1999. It was called wireless application protocol (WAP). WAP allowed mobile

Later editions of Snake included color and more detailed graphics.

devices to send and receive information over wireless **networks**. This revolutionized **software** applications by allowing apps to communicate on the internet. The first cell phones with WAP **browsers** came out in the early 2000s.

CHAPTER 6

THE iPHONE EFFECT

Cell phone companies continued to include apps on their phones. But apps really took off when Apple introduced the iPhone in 2007. It came loaded with several apps created by the company's app developers.

The apps on the iPhone included YouTube, Google Maps, email, a music player, and a calendar. These were native apps. Native apps are included on a device's OS and work only on that OS. The iPhone was also the first cell phone that had a fully functioning web **browser**.

Steve Jobs announced the first iPhone at Macworld, an annual expo for Apple products. More than six million original iPhones were sold!

Soon, people wanted apps for everything. But Apple didn't let developers outside the company build native apps for the iPhone's OS (iOS). Instead, people could build web-based apps using **techniques** such as Web 2.0 and Ajax. However, a group known as the jailbreaking community found ways to build and add native apps to the iPhone.

Apple wanted more control over the apps that were developed for the iPhone. So, the company decided to help people build native iOS apps. In March 2008, Apple released a **software** development kit. Now anyone could create apps for the iPhone. Four months later, Apple opened an **online** App Store. Developers could submit the apps they created to the store. If Apple accepted an app, people could purchase and **download** it.

APPLE APP STORE

When Apple first opened the App Store, it had about 550 apps. Today, it has more than two million. App developers earn 70 percent of the profits from the sales of their apps. Apple keeps the other 30 percent. An early popular app was the game Super Monkey Ball. In its first month, it was downloaded 300,000 times. This earned more than $2 million for Japanese video game company Sega.

CHAPTER 7
MORE MARKETS

Apple's App Store was not the only place to buy and sell apps. It, and the iPhone, soon got some competition. In November 2007, Google announced a partnership with nearly three dozen other **technology** and telecommunications companies. Some of these companies were HTC, Samsung, Motorola, and Sprint.

In October 2008, this partnership released the first Android smartphone. It was originally called the HTC Dream. It was later known as the T-Mobile G1. App developers hurried to design **software** for it.

Like Apple, Android gave app developers the tools to build apps for its phones. Apps for Android phones were **available** from the **online** app store Android Market. At first, the Android Market had around 50 apps. But within

DIGITAL BIT

By 2017, app developers had launched a combined total of nearly 5 million apps on Google Play and the Apple App Store.

The T-Mobile G1 cost $179. This was more than $300 cheaper than the first iPhone.

two years, there were more than 80,000 apps on the Android Market. In 2012, Android Market's name changed to Google Play.

While iOS apps are only **available** from the Apple App Store, there are several marketplaces for Android apps. Besides Google Play, two others include the Microsoft Store and Amazon Appstore. These have more than 600,000 apps each. And there is a high demand for Android and iOS app developers to keep coming up with new ideas.

CHAPTER 8
APP SUCCESS

Today, the iOS and Android marketplaces offer millions of apps. With so many apps **available**, it's hard for a new app to get noticed. It's not enough for an app developer to think an idea is great or useful. To make an app successful, an app developer must do research to make sure the app he or she wants to create is one that people will want or use.

The first step is to find out whether there are already similar apps available. If there are, the developer decides if his or her idea is different enough to be worth building. Perhaps it could be easier to use, have more features, or cost less than the other apps.

If there are no similar apps, the developer tries to learn why. Is it because people don't need or want the features the app will offer? The developer can use surveys to find out. These could show that people don't need or want the app. In that case, the developer may not build it. Ideally, the research will show that

Facebook is the most-used app on smartphones. The app can also be used on tablets and even televisions!

the idea is new and that people will want to use it. Then the developer can get to work building the app.

The work to make an app successful does not end once the app is built. Part of developing a successful app is creating a **marketing** plan. This includes how much to charge for the app. It also includes how to let people know that the app exists and where to **download** it.

Some app developers post ads on **social media** to spread the word about their app. Others offer their app for free. They hope many people will use it so the developers can make money selling ads, **upgrades**, and special features.

Many of the most successful apps can be used on more than one type of device.

One of the best-selling game apps of all time is Angry Birds. In 2009, **mobile** game company Rovio wanted to develop an iPhone app. Jaakko Iisalo was one of Rovio's game designers. He created a funny-looking flock of birds on his computer.

The Rovio team planned a game based around the bird characters. Angry Birds was released on the Apple App Store in 2010. Angry Birds became extremely popular almost immediately. It seemed everyone was playing it!

Within two years, the game had been **downloaded** 50 million times. Rovio has since launched 15 Angry Birds spin-off games. All together, these games have been downloaded more than three billion times.

There are also Angry Birds toys, clothes, costumes, and more. There was even an Angry Birds movie released in 2016. A **sequel** is planned for 2019.

CHAPTER 9
APP FUTURE

App development has started moving beyond general game, lifestyle, and entertainment apps. To do this, it is important for app developers to keep up to date with the latest **technology** and trends. As new technologies become **available**, app developers can use them to make new and better apps.

One trend is virtual reality. This is technology that creates artificial **environments** that a user can enter and interact with. **Augmented** reality is similar to virtual reality. But it adds artificial objects to users' real environments.

Wearables are another wave of the future for app developers. Computers keep getting smaller and smaller. As a result, they can be put into tiny devices that people can wear. Already, people can wear computers on their wrists, inside their glasses, or even as part of their clothing. Google Glass, Samsung Galaxy Gear, and Apple Watch are just a few examples of these types of

The popular app Pokémon GO uses augmented reality to show Pokémon characters in the user's environment.

wearables. And these wearables have apps that let them work with devices such as computers and smartphones.

It's possible that desktop computers will become a thing of the past. New **technology** is always being developed and replacing old devices. It's hard to imagine what devices and apps will be like in the future. But it's certain that app developers will play a big role in shaping them!

TIMELINE

1980s
The first PDAs are released with simple apps.

1997
Nokia offers a new cell phone with the game Snake.

1990s
Cell phones with apps are introduced.

2000
Cell phones with WAP browsers become available.

2007
The first Apple iPhone is released.

MARCH 2008

Apple releases a software development kit to help people develop iOS apps.

2010

The Angry Birds app becomes available on the Apple App Store.

JULY 2008

Apple opens the Apple App Store.

OCTOBER 2008

The first Android phone is released. The Android Market opens.

2017

Google Play and the Apple App Store reach nearly 5 million apps combined.

GLOSSARY

augmented–made greater, larger, or more complete.

available–able to be had or used.

breakthrough–a sudden advance or successful development.

browser–a computer program that is used to find and look at information on the Internet.

code–a set of instructions for a computer.

collaborate–to work with another person or group in order to do something or reach a goal.

download–to transfer data from a computer network to a single computer or device.

environment–surroundings.

feedback–information or criticism that suggests ways to improve something.

graphic–of or relating to visual arts such as painting and photography.

graphics–pictures or images on the screen of a computer, smartphone, or other device.

hardware–the physical parts of a computer.

lifestyle–the way a being, group, or society lives.

marketing–the process of advertising or promoting something so people will want to buy it.

mobile–capable of moving or being moved.

network–a system of computers connected by communications lines.

online–connected to the internet.

sequel–a book or a movie that continues the story of a previous book or movie.

social media–forms of electronic communication that allow people to create online communities to share information, ideas, messages. Facebook, Instagram, and Snapchat are examples of social media.

software–the written programs used to operate a computer.

specialize–to pursue one type of work, called a specialty. A person who does this is a specialist.

technique (tehk-NEEK)–a method or style in which something is done.

technology (tehk-NAH-luh-jee)–machinery and equipment developed for practical purposes using scientific principles and engineering.

upgrade–an occurrence in which one thing is replaced by something better, newer, or more valuable.

INDEX

Ajax, 19
Amazon, 12, 21
Android, 10, 13, 20, 21, 22
Angry Birds, 5, 25
Apple, 10, 13, 18, 19, 20, 21, 22, 25, 26
Armanto, Taneli, 16
augmented reality, 26

Blockade, 16
browsers, 5, 11, 17, 18

cell phones, 5, 10, 14, 16, 17, 18, 19, 20, 25, 27
collaborating, 5, 7, 12
communication, 12
computer memory, 16
computers, 5, 6, 8, 10, 14, 16, 26, 27
creativity, 6

Firefox, 11

games, 6, 14, 16, 25, 26
Google, 5, 10, 11, 12, 18, 20, 21, 26
graphic design, 7, 12

HTC, 20
HTML5, 11

Iisalo, Jaakko, 25
integrated development environments, 13
internet, 11, 17
iPhones, 18, 19, 20, 25

Java, 10

marketing, 24
Microsoft, 10, 21
mobile devices, 5, 6, 10, 16, 17
Motorola, 20

native apps, 18, 19
Nokia, 14, 16

operating systems, 10, 14, 16, 18, 19

personal digital assistants, 14
planning, 6, 8, 24, 25
Python, 10

Rovio, 25

Safari, 11
Samsung, 20, 26
Snake, 16
social media, 24
software, 5, 6, 10, 13, 16, 17, 19, 20
Spotify, 10
Sprint, 20

T-Mobile G1, 20
testing, 6, 8, 9, 13

virtual reality, 26

wearables, 26, 27
Web 2.0, 19
web-based apps, 11, 19
wireless application protocol, 16, 17

YouTube, 5, 10, 18